Seniors Sign, Too!

ASL FAMILY BOOK #2

Empowering Older Adults with an Alternative Voice Promoting Healthy Aging After Hearing Loss

Dr. D'YANN ELAINE D. DIV., M.ED, MAOM

Illustrated in American Sign Language by Filip Heyninck

COPYRIGHT

Publisher's Cataloging-in-Publication data

NAMES: Elaine, Dr. D'yann, author. | Heyninck, Filip, illustrator.

TITLE: *Seniors sign , too ! ASL family , book 2 , illustrated in American Sign Language :
empowering older adults with an alternative voice , promoting healthy aging after hearing loss* /
by Dr. D'yann Elaine; illustrated by Filip Heyninck.

SERIES: Seniors, Sign Too!

DESCRIPTION: Los Angeles, CA: Dr. D'yann Elaine, 2023.

IDENTIFIERS: LCCN: 2022923454 | ISBN: 979-8-9861021-3-9 (hardcover) | 979-8-9861021-4-6 (paperback) |
979-8-9861021-5-3 (e-Book)

SUBJECTS: LCSH American Sign Language.| Sign language--Handbooks, manuals, etc. | Older people. | Hearing disorders. | Older deaf people. | BISAC LANGUAGE ARTS & DISCIPLINES / Sign Language | SELF-HELP /
Aging | FAMILY & RELATIONSHIPS / Life Stages / Later Years | FAMILY & RELATIONSHIPS / Eldercare

CLASSIFICATION: LCC HV2474 .D93 2023 | DDC 419--dc23

DEDICATION

I dedicate this book with love, admiration,
and gratitude for the people in my life:

To my jewel, my daughter, my inspiration, A. Brytney Reaves.

To my parents, Larry and Leeaada Dorsey,
for always loving me and teaching me how to love, and for supporting
me and choosing me against many odds. I love you eternally.

To the beautiful people of the Deaf community, with my humble
appreciation. Thank you for embracing me as an ally and entrusting
me to share your treasured language, a vivid canvas of exquisite
expressions. I am honored to support ASL awareness and stand
with you for diversity, equality and inclusion for individuals
who are Deaf and hard-of-hearing in all settings and industry.
I pray the world will see ASL for what it is: a rich and expressive
cognitive delight that unites humans, instills peace, builds
relationships, making our world a better place for all mankind.

INTRODUCTION

Welcome to the most unique and entertaining ASL Illustrated book ever! Written with the aging adult perspective in mind, this book is #2 of twelve in the series and is a perfect way for older adults aged 55+ to engage in sign language as an alternative visual communication tool. Connect your favorite elder with grandchildren, sons and daughters, friends, and caretakers by putting language in their hands. The series features an illustrated cast of characters and a delightful interplay between letters and drawings. This combination brings nostalgic memories to mind while seamlessly connecting with today's reality.

Whether young, old or in between, you are invited to join our HearZero community of signers to empower older adults with a way to communicate visually when it becomes more challenging to express thoughts with words.

Welcome

WHO DO YOU LOVE?

ABOVE ALL,
*keep loving one
another earnestly,
since love covers
a multitude of sins.*

1 Peter 4:8 ESV

Family
like branches on a tree,
we all grow in different directions,
yet our roots remain as one.
~ Anonymous

I LOVE FAMILY

FAMILY

Grandchildren

ARE THE CROWN OF

THE ELDERLY, AND THE

GLORY OF CHILDREN

IS THEIR PARENTS.

PROVERBS 17:6 CEB

I LOVE GRANDPARENTS

GRANDMA

GRANDPA

Children

are a blessing

and a gift

from the Lord.

Psalms 127:3 CEV

I LOVE GRANDDAUGHTER & SON

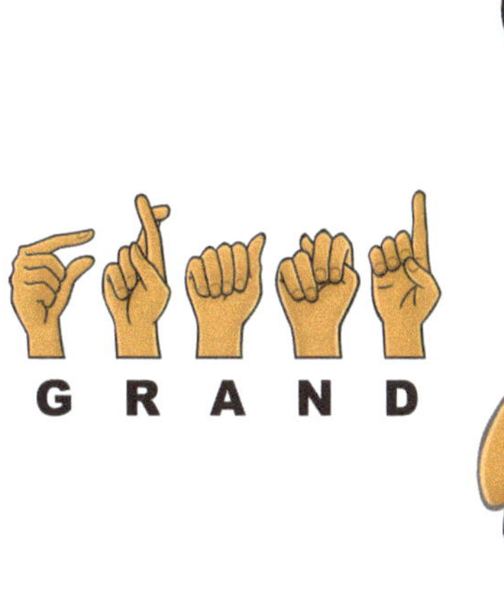

G R A N D

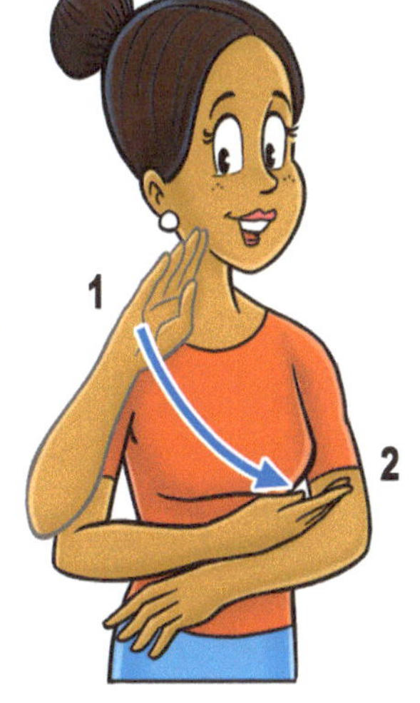

DAUGHTER

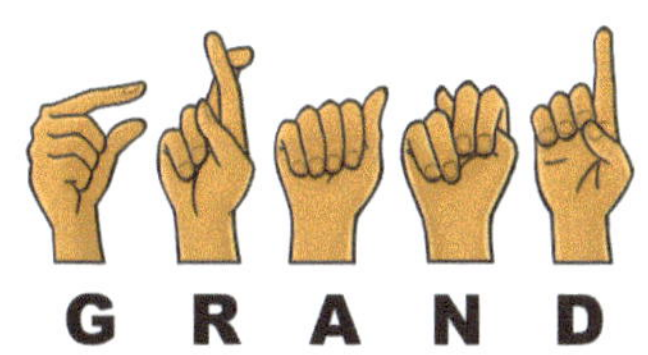

G R A N D

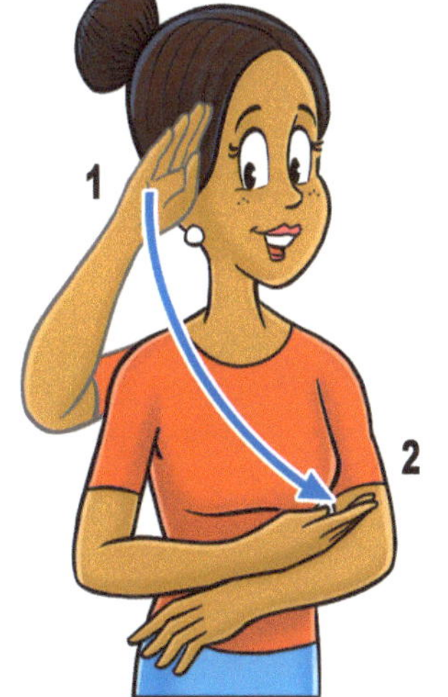

SON

Always be

HUMBLE AND GENTLE.
PATIENTLY PUT UP WITH EACH OTHER
AND LOVE EACH OTHER.

Ephesians 4:2 CEV

I LOVE HUSBAND & WIFE

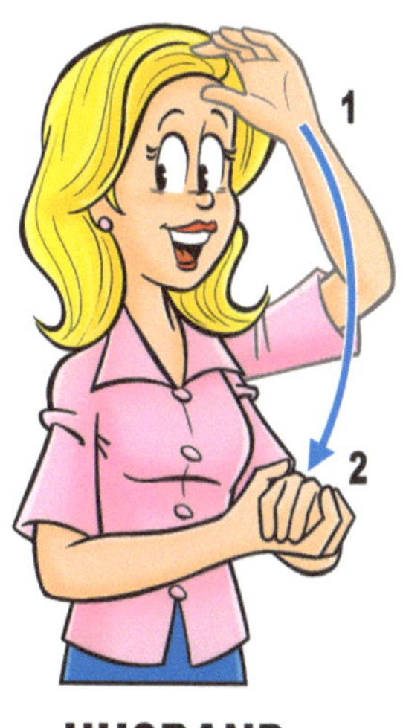

HUSBAND

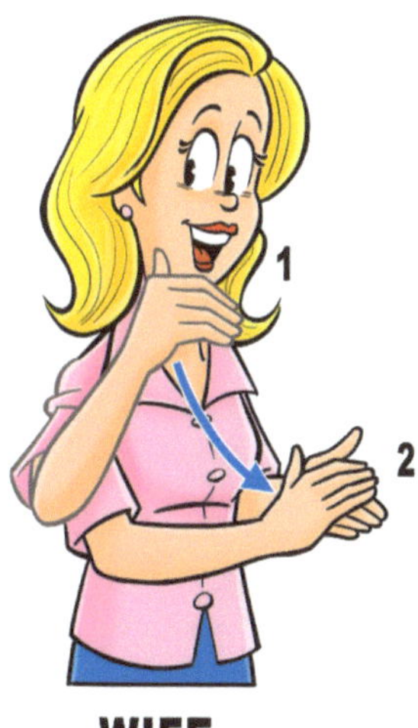

WIFE

Nobody on earth
can ever love you
more than your parents.

~ Anonymous

I LOVE MOM & DAD

MOM

DAD

Your *wife* will be as fruitful,

as a grapevine, and just

as an *olive* tree

is rich with olives,

your home will be rich

with healthy *children*.

Psalm 128:3
CEV

I LOVE DAUGHTER & SON

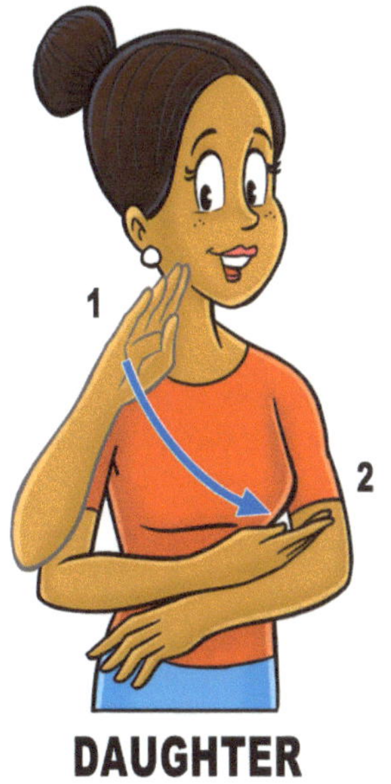

DAUGHTER

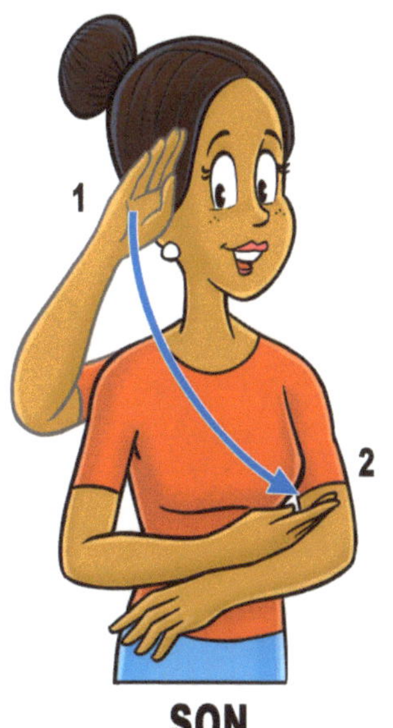

SON

They say that
no matter how old you become,
when you are with your siblings,
you revert back to childhood.

~ Anonymous

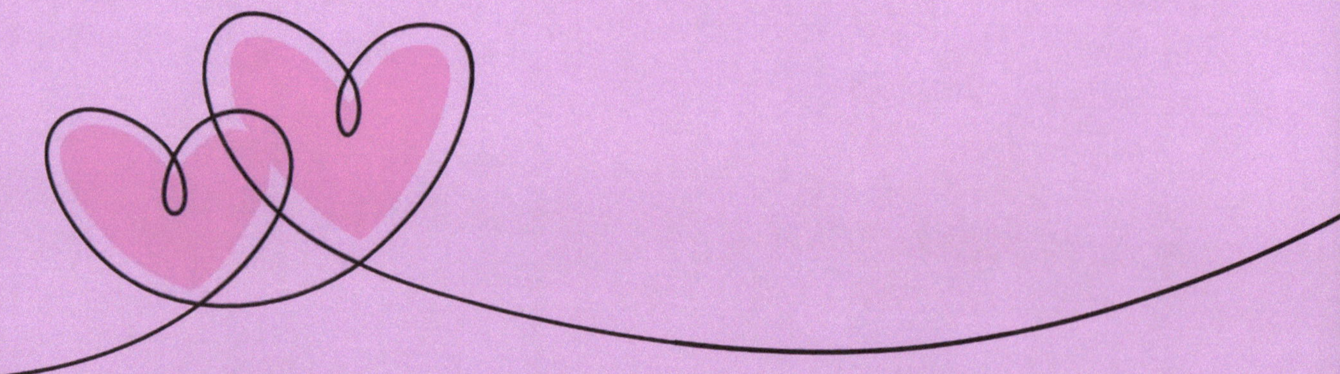

I LOVE SISTER & BROTHER

Honor
(respect, obey, care for)
your *father* and your *mother*,
so that your days may
be prolonged in the land the
lord your *God* gives you.

Exodus 20:12 CEV

Respect
your *father* and your *mother*,
and you will live a long time
in the land I am giving you.

Exodus 20:12 CEV

I LOVE CHILDREN

CHILDREN

SOMETIMES THE BEST MEDICINE IS UNCONDITIONAL LOVE FROM YOUR PET.

~ Anonymous

I LOVE PETS

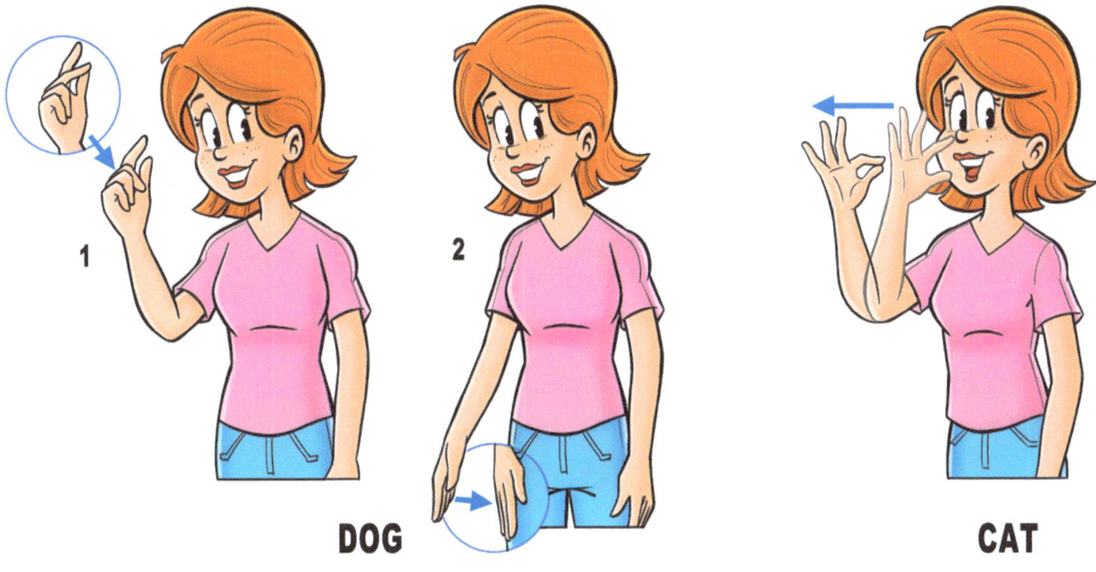

BE
Jealous
I have
the BEST
Aunt &
Uncle!
~ Anonymous

I LOVE AUNT & UNCLE

AUNT

UNCLE

If nephews and
NIECES
were Jewels,

I WOULD HAVE THE MOST

Beautiful Gems

EVER.

~ Anonymous

NIECE & NEPHEW

NIECE

NEPHEW

LOVE *is patient is kind.*

It bears all things, believes all things, hopes all things, endures all things. **Love never fails.**

1 Corinthians 13:4-8 CEV

I LOVE FRIENDS

flip

FRIEND

Family isn't
always blood. It's the
people in your life who
want you in theirs;
the ones who accept
you for who you are.
The ones who would
do anything to see
you smile & who

no matter what.

~ Anonymous

I LOVE CHURCH FAMILY

You are altogether
Beautiful,
my love; there is
no flaw in YOU.

Song of Solomon 4:7 ESV

I LOVE MYSELF

MYSELF

... **Love**

each other.

Love

comes from **God** ...

1 John 4:7 CEV

I LOVE YOU

ABOUT THE AUTHOR

DR. D'YANN ELAINE is a leading American Sign Language (ASL) educator, interpreter, consultant, author, producer, and the founder of Sign with Me, Inc.

DR. D'YANN ELAINE, D.DIV., M.ED., MAOM

She is an expert in connecting the hearing and Deaf communities and blazing new trails in this field.

Dr. D'yann was born in Watts and was a USC Women of Troy basketball player. She holds a Doctorate in Divinity, two Bachelor's and two Master's degrees from prestigious universities. With a passion for social equity and inclusion, Dr. D'yann's goal is to help people expand their perspectives and focus on their abilities instead of their limitations.

With over two decades of experience, Dr. D'yann has dedicated her life to teaching others. She is the executive producer of the ASL Emergency Preparedness DVD Series and Unheard Voices Talk Show, as well as the author of the *"Seniors Sign, Too!"* book series. Her vision is to inspire a new generation of signers and make a positive impact by unifying communities through language.

ABOUT THE ILLUSTRATOR

FILIP HEYNINCK is a renowned Deaf illustrator. He resides in Waasmunster, Belgium with his wife Katrien Van Laere, two adult hearing children (CODAs), Kimberly and Dalvin, one dog and two cats. Filip is a dedicated husband and father and an extraordinary cartoonist and illustrator. He has been drawing and creating visual artwork since he learned to hold a pencil as a toddler. His wife Katrien is a graphic designer who colors all his drawings and does the layout and administrative tasks. Together, Filip and Katrien are a dynamic duo.

FILIP HEYNINCK

Filip's work has occupied bookstore shelves since 2005 and includes comic books, such as Visual Box's *Deaf Pinocchio*, *Deaf Devils*, and *Slim Gezien*, which inspired his own first comic book publications: *The *S.P.O.R.T.S.: Gold...Set! Match!*, *Otherworldly Game*, and *Ninia Dance Battle*.

Website: http://www.filipheyninck.com, Email: filip.heyninck1@telenet.be, Social Media: FB, IG @filipheyninck

ABOUT THE TEAM

KATHLEEN MARCATH has a B.A. degree in Deaf Community Studies from Madonna University. She is a children's book author whose interest in ASL escalated when she learned to sign the song, *Our God Is an Awesome God*. The beauty and power of ASL captured her attention and never let go. Countless times, she has watched the same magic illuminate other people's faces (deaf and hearing alike) when they learn this beautiful language. Her goal is to promote ASL literacy and raise awareness of its importance to audiences of all ages and backgrounds. In 2020, she founded ASL Picture Books to address the lack of representation of Deaf culture in children's books, and published her award-winning debut children's book, *My Monster Truck Goes Everywhere With Me*. A senior herself, Kathleen is proud to be the project manager for the *Seniors Sign, Too!* series.

KATHLEEN MARCATH

Website: https://www.aslpicturebooks.com, Email: info@aslpicturebooks.com, Social Media: FB, IG @aslpicturebooks 

DEBBIE RISH-GREEN

DEBBIE RISH-GREEN is a Los Angeles native and community networker with a B.A. degree in Business Management and two associates degrees. She is the author of *Rocky the Clown*, the executive producer of *Africa In My Veins*, collaborator author of *Marriage Ain't Fa Punks*, and co-project manager, director and co-writer of the *Seniors Sign, Too!* video series. Debbie found her new love for the Deaf community in her role as key production assistant on the *Unheard Voices Season 1* talk show project. She is a certified instructor of English as a Foreign Language (TEFL) and teaches international students online. Debbie is a dedicated wife, mother, and pastor.

Email: rockytheclownfan@gmail.com, Social Media: Facebook @rockytheclown, IG @thecoolestclown

COMING SOON!

VIDEOS
CLASSES
MOBILE APP
TRAINING
WORK BOOKS
COLORING BOOK
FLASHCARDS
FOLLOW US
SUBSCRIBE TO OUR MAILING LIST
www.signwithme.org

THANK YOU!

CONTACT
Sign with Me, Incorporated

@signwithmeorg
www.signwithme.org
Email: hearzerosales@signwithme.org
Phone: (310) 362-8290
VP (213) 647-3903

*Partial proceeds from sales support ASL education, deaf institutions and organizations.

SUPPORT ACCESSIBLE MEDIA WITH A DONATION TODAY!

SPECIAL THANKS

My sincerest thanks to all those who made this vision manifest.
I love and appreciate you all for your contributions
and believing in our vision!

ASL ALPHABET

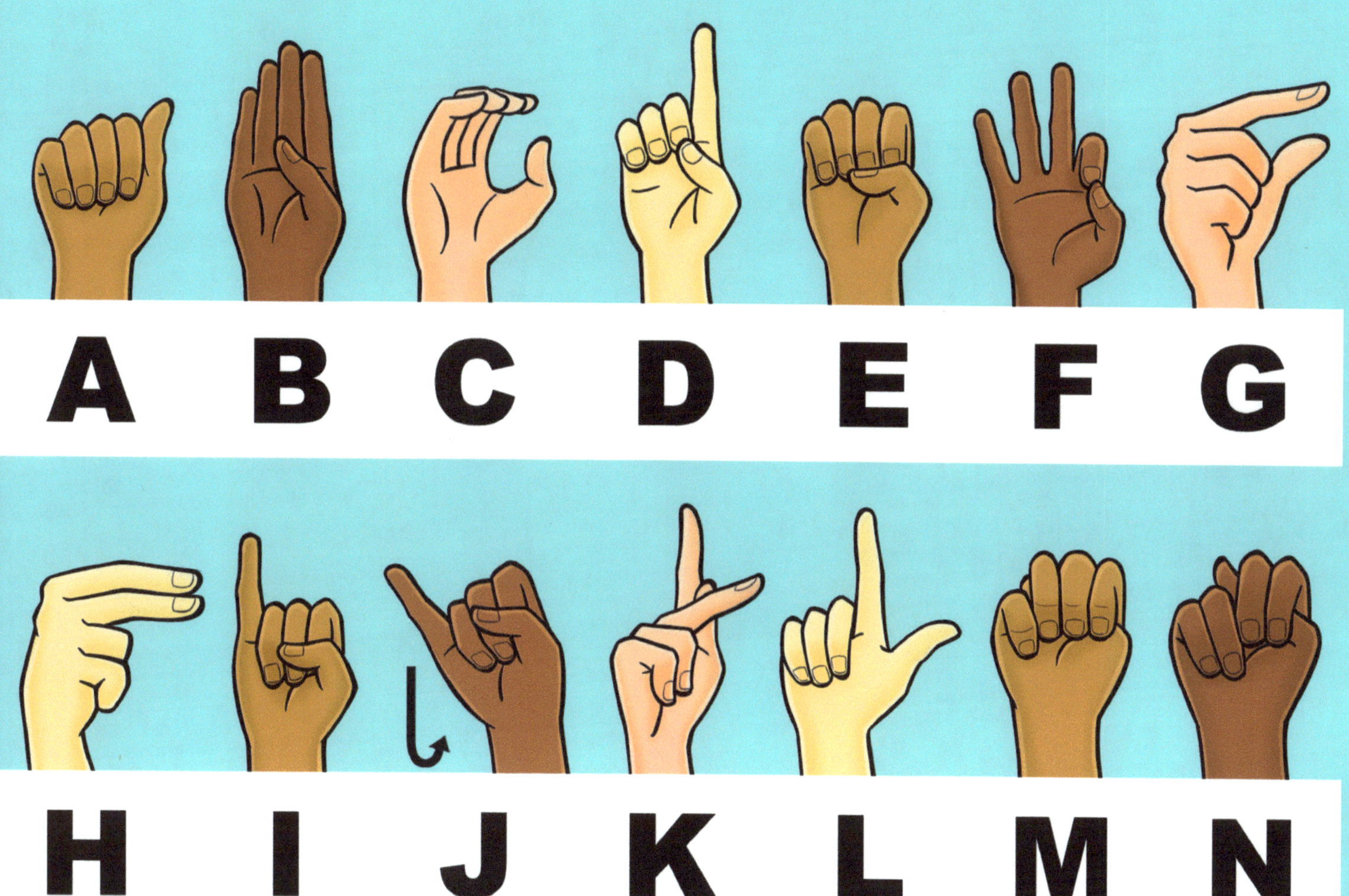

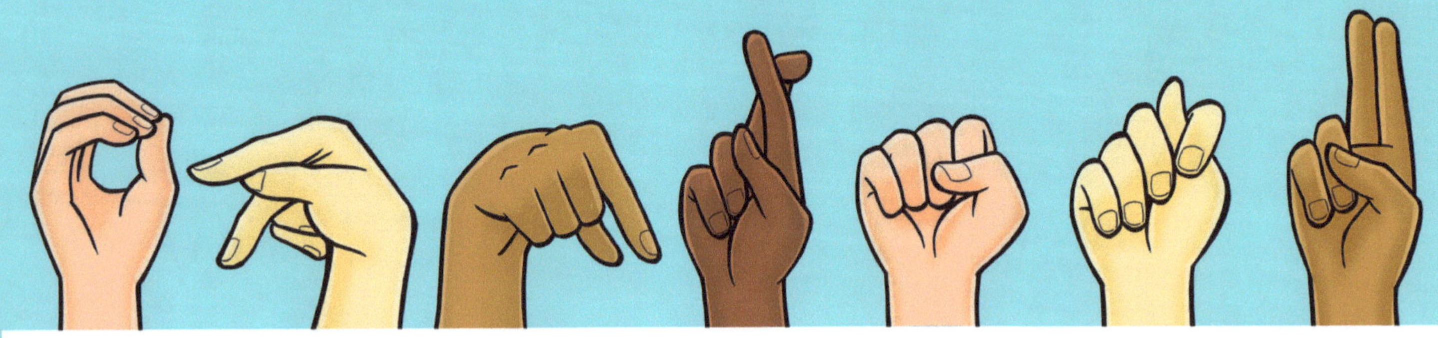

O P Q R S T U

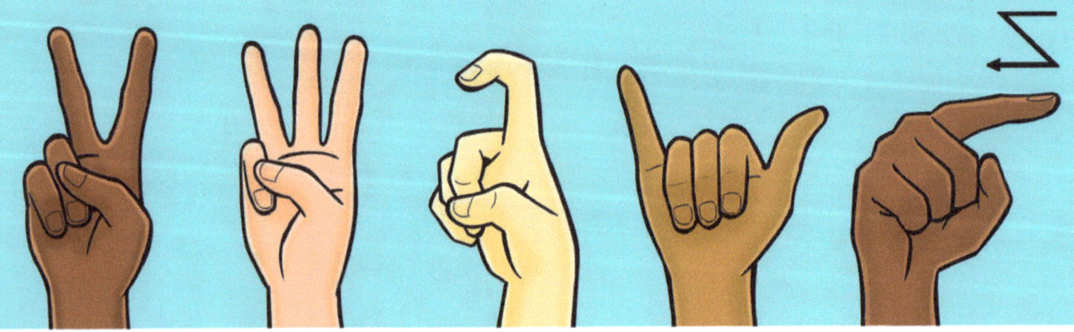

V W X Y Z

MEET THE CHARACTERS

MEET THE CHARACTERS CONT.

LANGUAGE MODELS

GLOSSARY

WHO

YOU

LOVE

FAMILY

GRANDMA

GRANDPA

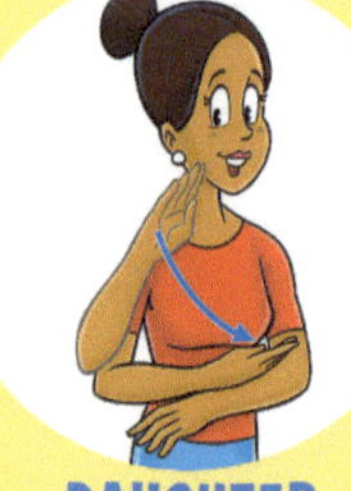

DAUGHTER

SON

HUSBAND

WIFE

DAD

MOM

SISTER

BROTHER

CHILDREN

DOG

CAT

AUNT

UNCLE

NIECE

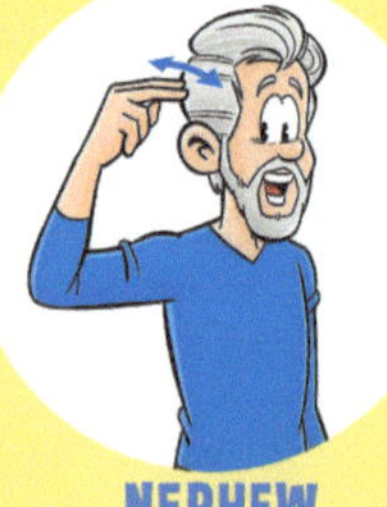

NEPHEW

FRIEND

CHURCH

MYSELF

www.ingramcontent.com/pod-product-compliance
Lightning Source LLC
Chambersburg PA
CBHW041605110726
48005CB00002B/293